Ownership of Trademarks

Copyright Statement

Dedication

ODIN

LEO

This book is dedicated to the dogs of the Test Innovators office, who consistently inspire us with their perseverance, their ability to learn new things, and their unparalleled enthusiasm.

MERCY

BECKY

Table of Contents

ACKNOWLEDGMENTS..3

CHAPTER 1: AN OVERVIEW OF THE ISEE..5

CHAPTER 2: THE SECTIONS OF THE ISEE.....................................21

CHAPTER 3: PREPARING FOR THE ISEE.......................................29

CHAPTER 4: STRATEGIES FOR THE ISEE......................................35

    VERBAL...38

    MATH...42

    READING 46

    ESSAY...48

CHAPTER 5: CONCLUSION...51

Acknowledgments

This book contains the collective knowledge of the Test Innovators team, a group of educators and technology experts dedicated to helping students succeed on standardized tests.

Special thanks to Edan Shahar, Erin Lynch, Geoff Dennis, Joshua Dolim, and Marina Flider, PhD for their editorial wisdom, and to Rebecca Caldera for beautiful design elements.

About Us

We at Test Innovators believe that standardized test taking is a skill you can learn, and mastering this skill can open doors to new opportunities throughout your life.

Our decades of experience with test writing and teaching, combined with our dedication to finding the best technological solutions, provide students with an unparalleled test preparation experience.

We believe that with the right tools, a personalized learning path, plenty of practice, and support throughout the process, every student can reach their fullest potential and find the test preparation process fulfilling rather than stressful.

Chapter 1:

An Overview of the ISEE

What is the ISEE?

The ISEE (Independent Schools Entrance Exam) is an admission test administered by the ERB (Educational Records Bureau). Many private schools in North America, and a handful of international schools, use the ISEE as a crucial part of the admissions process for grades 2 through 12.

The ISEE serves as a standardized metric by which admissions departments can compare students from different schools. There are many parts to an application, and the manner in which ISEE scores impact admissions is very school-dependent.

Regardless of the school, an excellent score on the ISEE sets you apart in the admissions process, especially at highly competitive schools. Based on our years of test prep experience, we believe that standardized test taking is a skill that you can master, and — like all skills — you need to learn and practice in order to improve.

This book will serve as your guide in the preparation process, giving you insights into the test as well as strategies that will allow you to tackle the ISEE with confidence.

Is the ISEE related to the ERBs that I took?

If you already attend an independent school, you may have taken the Comprehensive Testing Program (CTP), which is commonly referred to as the ERBs. The CTP, like the ISEE, is developed by the ERB. However, the CTP is an achievement test administered by schools to assess their students' current skills, whereas the ISEE is an admission test.

Scores on the CTPs and other achievement tests are often higher than ISEE scores. Achievement tests are designed to measure a student's grade-level proficiency in a subject, while admission tests like the ISEE are designed to compare many potentially qualified applicants.

Levels of the ISEE

The ISEE has four test levels, each of which is taken by students applying to a range of grades.

Primary Level

Primary Level 2
For application to grade 2

Primary Level 3
For application to grade 3

Primary Level 4
For application to grade 4

Lower Level

For application to grades 5 or 6

Middle Level

For application to grades 7 or 8

Upper Level

For application to grades 9 - 12

It might seem like a disadvantage for a younger student to be taking the same test as older students, but it's a little more complicated.

The ISEE is scored based on the grade for which a student is applying, so students are **only compared to others applying to the same grade.**

So, a student applying to grade 9 will not be competing against a student who is two years older, applying to grade 11.

However, an 8th grader will be taking a test with questions designed to identify the top 11th graders. Knowing not to dwell on these difficult questions is critical to success on the ISEE.

ISEE Timing and Structure

The number of questions and timing varies for each level of the ISEE.

Primary Level 2 ISEE:

For application to grade 2

SECTION	QUESTIONS	TIME
Auditory Comprehension	6 questions	7 minutes
Reading	18 questions	20 minutes
Break	–	5 minutes
Mathematics	24 questions	26 minutes
Writing Sample*	1 picture prompt	Untimed
TOTAL	**49 questions**	**58 minutes + writing**

Primary Level 3 ISEE:

For application to grade 3

SECTION	QUESTIONS	TIME
Reading	24 questions	28 minutes
Break	–	5 minutes
Mathematics	24 questions	26 minutes
Writing Sample*	1 picture prompt	Untimed
TOTAL	**49 questions**	**59 minutes + writing**

Primary Level 4 ISEE:

For application to grade 4

SECTION	QUESTIONS	TIME
Reading	28 questions	30 minutes
Break	–	5 minutes
Mathematics	28 questions	30 minutes
Writing Sample*	1 prompt	Untimed
TOTAL	**57 questions**	**65 minutes + writing**

*Note: the primary level writing sample is not administered to New York City test takers.

Lower Level ISEE:
For application to grades 5 or 6

SECTION	QUESTIONS	TIME
Verbal Reasoning	34 questions	20 minutes
Quantitative Reasoning	38 questions	35 minutes
Break	–	5-10 minutes
Reading Comprehension	25 questions	25 minutes
Mathematics Achievement	30 questions	30 minutes
Break	–	5-10 minutes
Essay	1 prompt	30 minutes
TOTAL	**128 questions**	**2 hours, 30 minutes**

Middle Level ISEE:
For application to grades 7 or 8

SECTION	QUESTIONS	TIME
Verbal Reasoning	40 questions	20 minutes
Quantitative Reasoning	37 questions	35 minutes
Break	–	5-10 minutes
Reading Comprehension	36 questions	35 minutes
Mathematics Achievement	47 questions	40 minutes
Break	–	5-10 minutes
Essay	1 prompt	30 minutes
TOTAL	**161 questions**	**2 hours, 50 minutes**

Upper Level ISEE:
For application to grades 9 - 12

SECTION	QUESTIONS	TIME
Verbal Reasoning	40 questions	20 minutes
Quantitative Reasoning	37 questions	35 minutes
Break	–	5-10 minutes
Reading Comprehension	36 questions	35 minutes
Mathematics Achievement	47 questions	40 minutes
Break	–	5-10 minutes
Essay	1 prompt	30 minutes
TOTAL	**161 questions**	**2 hours, 50 minutes**

Test Format

The ISEE is administered in two formats.

Paper test

Computer test

Most school testing sites administer the test on paper, although a few administer the computer version. Students may also take the test on a computer at a Prometric center.

Students taking the ISEE on paper will write the essay in blue or black ink. Students taking the ISEE on a computer will type the essay.

Note: the Primary Level ISEE is only administered on computers.

Should I take the test on a computer or on paper?

If you have the choice, here are some things to consider:

The environment: Students taking the test at a Prometric center may be sitting next to a whole range of students all taking different tests (say, a 22-year-old college student taking the GRE). At a school testing site, every student will be roughly the same age and there to take the ISEE. Consider how these two different environments might impact you.

The essay: Students taking the ISEE on a computer will type the essay. For slow typists, this might be difficult. Students taking the test on paper will write the essay out by hand. For students who have trouble writing legibly, this might present a challenge. Consider which format will be more advantageous for you.

The answer sheet: Many students have trouble correctly bubbling their answers into an answer sheet. They may skip a question but forget to skip that line on their bubble sheet. On the computer test, this is not an issue: students enter each answer on the same screen as the question.

Our advice: Take a practice test both ways, see which one goes better, and sign up accordingly.

ISEE Question Types

There are two types of questions on the ISEE. Every section of the ISEE, except the essay or writing sample, consists of multiple-choice questions with four answer choices. They look like this:

> How many answer choices do ISEE questions have?
> (A) 1
> (B) 2
> (C) 3
> (D) 4

Students indicate the answer (hopefully D in this case) on their answer sheets, bubbling in their choice.

The essay section requires students to write a response to the given prompt. These prompts might look something like this:

> Who is one of your favorite characters from a book, and why?

Students taking the Primary Level 2 and Primary Level 3 will receive a picture prompt rather than a written prompt. A picture prompt presents students with a picture and asks them to write a story about what they see.

ISEE Scoring

Admissions departments and parents usually talk about ISEE scores in terms of stanines. For each section of the test, except for the unscored essay section, students receive a stanine score from 1 through 9. Since stanines are a normalized score (more about that on the next page), they depend only on how a student performed compared to others applying to the same grade.

Here's an example of what an ISEE score report looks like. At the top of the report, you'll see overall scores for each section of the test:

Section	Scaled Score (760 – 940)	Percentile Rank (1 – 99)	Stanine (1 – 9)	Stanine Analysis 1 2 3 4 5 6 7 8 9
Verbal Reasoning	847	26	4	■V■
Reading Comprehension	856	40	5	■R■
Quantitative Reasoning	860	33	4	■Q■
Mathematics Achievement	867	40	5	■M■

Note that although percentiles provide more specific information about how a student's performance compared to others of the same age, the most commonly referenced ISEE scores are still the stanines.

Underneath the overall scores on the score report, you will see a more detailed breakdown. Each section is broken into question types, and to the right, + signs and - signs indicate which questions were answered correctly and incorrectly.

ISEE sections are ordered by difficulty, except for the reading section, and the score report reflects this. Thus, the first question within a subsection was the easiest one, and the last question was the hardest. Score reports show whether students missed easy questions (toward the beginning of a subsection) or harder questions (toward the end).

Section & Subsection	# of Questions	# Correct	Results for Each Question
Verbal Reasoning			
Synonyms	16	9	+- ++++++++- - - +- - -
Single Word Response	19	8	- - - +- ++- +- - - ++- - - ++
Quantitative Reasoning			
Word Problems	18	5	- - - +- +- - +- - +- +- - - -
Quantitative Comparisons	14	10	- +- - ++++++- +++
Reading Comprehension			
Main Idea	5	4	++- ++
Supporting Ideas	6	4	++- ++-
Inference	6	4	+++- +-
Vocabulary	6	3	+++- - -
Organization/Logic	4	2	- +- +
Tone/Style/Figurative Language	3	1	+- -
Mathematics Achievement			
Whole Numbers	8	6	++- +++- +
Decimals, Percents, Fractions	8	4	+- +- - - ++
Algebraic Concepts	9	2	- +- - +- - - -
Geometry	5	3	+++- -
Measurement	5	1	- - - +-
Data Analysis and Probability	7	4	+++- - +-

LEGEND: + = Correct - = Incorrect S = Skipped N = Not Reached

Score Report Insights

Here is a breakdown of the different scores presented on the ISEE score report, and their importance:

Scaled Score: The scaled score for each section is a number between 760 and 940. This contains the same information as the percentile, but in a less straightforward way. Focus on the percentile instead.

Percentile Rank: This is the best number to use to understand student performance, and relates directly to the stanine (explained below), which is the measure that schools primarily use.

The percentile compares a student's performance to all other same-grade students taking the same test. For example, a 20th percentile indicates that a student answered more questions correctly than 20% of students applying to the same grade.

Stanine: The primary numbers referenced by schools to describe ISEE scores are the stanines. Each stanine correlates to a percentile range, as shown in this chart:

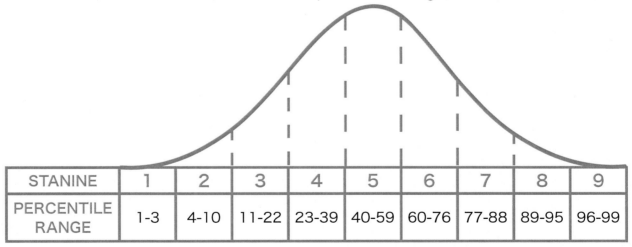

STANINE	1	2	3	4	5	6	7	8	9
PERCENTILE RANGE	1-3	4-10	11-22	23-39	40-59	60-76	77-88	89-95	96-99

Notice that the percentile ranges for the middle stanines of 4-6 are far larger than the ranges for the extreme stanines of 1, 2, 8, or 9. This means that most students taking the ISEE achieve scores in the middle range. Only the top 3 percent of all test takers receive a stanine of 9 on any given section.

Raw Score: This simply indicates the number of questions a student answered correctly out of the total number of questions. This score is not very meaningful because, unlike on in-school tests where students are always aiming for a high percent of correct answers, on the ISEE, performance is all relative. On a hard test section, answering 50% of the questions could be great. The comparison with how other students did on each test section is all that matters.

Schools and ISEE Scores

The purpose of the ISEE is to provide school admissions panels with a standardized metric they can use to compare applicants from different schools. Because of this, it is a central part of the application. However, it is important to remember that it is just that: one part of the application. The transcript, interview, recommendations, essays, and other components of the application are all critical for successful applicants. That said, we have seen that low scores can be an obstacle to admissions, especially for competitive schools that receive a large number of applications.

The Test Innovators website displays data on score ranges that have historically made students competitive applicants at different schools. These are designed to provide directional information but are by no means absolute.

Here's what this school data looks like:

View this information for all of the schools you are interested in here:

https://ISEEpracticetest.com/content/schools

As you look through the information on your target schools, remember that there are many parts to an application. Scores in the green range do not guarantee admission, nor do scores in the red range preclude it.

Common Score Questions

How soon will I receive my score report?

You will be able to see your score report through your online account with ERB within about two weeks of the test date.

Can I see the score report before sending it to schools?

Yes! Especially if you test (or may test) more than once, we strongly recommend that you wait until you see the score report(s) before determining the schools to which you would like to send them.

If I test more than once, can I send only the best score for each section?

No. Though some schools may choose to do this as they review student score reports, the admissions offices will be able to see the complete score report for each test you choose to send.

Why are my ISEE scores lower than my usual standardized test scores?

ISEE test takers tend to be high performers, and a 50th percentile score means that you're testing right in the middle of this talented pack. The competitive nature of the test is, however, a very good reason to practice before sitting down for the official exam.

Registration Tips

Find testing dates in your area here: https://iseepracticetest.com/dates

Students can take the ISEE once per testing season:

 **FALL** Aug-Nov

 **WINTER** Dec-Mar

 **SPRING/SUMMER** Apr-Jul

When should I take the test?

Whenever possible, we recommend that you plan to be able to take the test twice. This helps alleviate the pressure of a single testing date, and if the first test goes well, you don't have to take it again.

This means that your first test date must be before the end of November (probably in October or November), and your second test date can be in December or January. Check the testing deadlines for the schools to which you're applying to make sure that you test in time. You will probably need to take the test by January, but there are occasional exceptions.

Register for the test here: https://www.erblearn.org/parents/isee-registration

Tip

When you register for the test, you will have the opportunity to enter the schools to which you would like to send your scores. Do not enter schools yet! There is no reason to send the scores BEFORE you have the opportunity to review the score report.

If you have a secondary school placement advisor, they may ask you to enter your current school so that they can best counsel you.

Accommodations

Some students are eligible for accommodations on the ISEE. Accommodations will not be visible on the ISEE score report sent to schools, so admissions offices will not know if a student took the test with accommodations.

To be eligible, students must have a documented learning difference or disability that requires accommodations and currently be receiving accommodations at their school for that need.

The most common accommodation on the ISEE is fifty percent additional time, but there are many others.

It may take **up to two weeks** for an accommodations request to be processed, and students must be approved before they can register for an ISEE test date with accommodations. Be sure to send in your documentation as soon as possible!

Register at https://www.erblearn.org/parents/isee-accommodations

Test Day Information

The day before the test, relax, read a book, get some exercise, and get plenty of sleep. (In fact, you should prioritize sleep the entire week before the test as those earlier nights' sleep will be critical.)

On the morning of the test, wake up with ample time to eat a good breakfast and head to the test center so that you arrive at (or before!) your check-in time.

Do not attempt to study or cram last-minute information on the night before or day of the test! This will only cause undue stress and anxiety. Now is the time to feel confident in everything you've already done to prepare.

What to bring to the test:

Verification Letter

Identification

A snack

Water

Verification Letter: This will be emailed to you when you register for the test and confirms the test date, time, and location.

Identification: Any of the following constitutes a valid form of identification: library card, birth certificate, social security card, school report card, school ID, passport, or green card.

For paper/pencil testing:

Four #2 pencils

Four erasers

Two pens with blue or black ink (for the essay)

Prohibited items:

Everything not listed on the previous page! This includes:

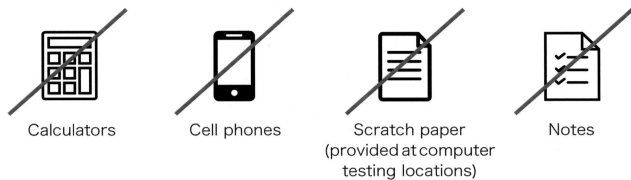

Calculators

Cell phones

Scratch paper
(provided at computer
testing locations)

Notes

Chapter 2:

The Sections of the ISEE

Verbal Reasoning

The Verbal Reasoning section of the ISEE is composed of two types of questions.

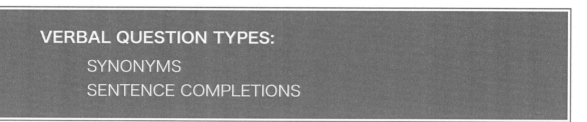

VERBAL QUESTION TYPES:
>   SYNONYMS
>   SENTENCE COMPLETIONS

The first half of the section is synonym questions, which look like this:

CELEBRATE
>   (A)   align
>   (B)   fathom
>   (C)   rejoice
>   (D)   salivate

Students are given a word and then asked to find its closest synonym in the answer choices.

The second half of the Verbal Reasoning section is sentence completion questions. Sentence completions look like this:

The farmers were wisely —— to use the damaged farm equipment.
>   (A)   desperate
>   (B)   eager
>   (C)   happy
>   (D)   hesitant

Students are given a sentence with a blank and asked to find the answer choice that best completes the sentence. Upper Level students will see questions with two blanks, and Lower Level students will see questions where a phrase is needed to complete the sentence, rather than just one word.

Quantitative Reasoning

The Quantitative Reasoning section is one of two math sections on the ISEE. This section focuses primarily on **problem-solving skills** and **critical thinking**. These types of problems frequently do not require significant calculation, but rather numerical and logical reasoning.

> **QUANTITATIVE REASONING SUBJECTS:**
> NUMBERS AND OPERATIONS
> ALGEBRA
> GEOMETRY
> MEASUREMENT
> DATA ANALYSIS AND PROBABILITY
> PROBLEM SOLVING

On the Lower Level ISEE, this section contains only word problems. For the Middle and Upper Levels of the test, there are two types of questions in the section: word problems and quantitative comparisons. Quantitative comparisons always have the same four answer choices, and look like this:

> Column A   Column B
> 1/2 of 60   1/3 of 100
>
> (A) The quantity in Column A is greater.
> (B) The quantity in Column B is greater.
> (C) The two quantities are equal.
> (D) The relationship cannot be determined
>   from the information given.

Reading Comprehension

In the Reading Comprehension section, students will be asked to read passages dealing with a variety of subjects.

> **READING PASSAGE SUBJECTS:**
>
> SCIENCE
> HISTORY
> ARTS
> CONTEMPORARY LIFE

They will then be asked to answer questions based on the information given in each passage. The Lower Level Reading Comprehension section has 5 passages with 5 questions each, and the Middle and Upper Level Reading Comprehension sections have 6 passages with 6 questions each. Students can expect to see a variety of different question types on this section.

> **READING QUESTION TYPES:**
>
> MAIN IDEA
> SUPPORTING IDEA
> INFERENCE
> VOCABULARY IN CONTEXT
> TONE/STYLE/FIGURATIVE LANGUAGE
> ORGANIZATION/LOGIC

Below is an example of an organization/logic question:

> Which best describes the organization of the passage?
> (A)   facts are followed by opinions
> (B)   an argument is stated and then defended
> (C)   events are outlined in chronological order
> (D)   a problem is presented and then possible solutions given

Mathematics Achievement

The Mathematics Achievement section is the second of the two math sections on the ISEE. While the Quantitative Reasoning section focuses on problem solving and mathematical reasoning, the Mathematics Achievement section focuses on **specific math content** and **skills taught in school**.

The general subjects covered on the Mathematics Achievement and Quantitative Reasoning sections, however, are the same:

> **MATHEMATICS ACHIEVEMENT SUBJECTS:**
> NUMBERS AND OPERATIONS
> ALGEBRA
> GEOMETRY
> MEASUREMENT
> DATA ANALYSIS AND PROBABILITY
> PROBLEM SOLVING

Unlike the Quantitative Reasoning section, the Mathematics Achievement section requires students to know mathematical terminology and to do more significant calculation.

Questions on the Mathematics Achievement section will look like this:

> Which of the following is equivalent to the expression shown below?
> $$\frac{5-10x\sqrt{81}}{\sqrt{25}}$$
> (A)   -90x
> (B)   1 - 90x
> (C)   1 - 18x
> (D)   5 - 18x

Essay

The essay section is the only unscored portion of the ISEE. A copy is sent to schools along with the score report.

Students will be asked to write an essay in response to the given prompt. Essay prompts will look like this:

> If you could take a class to learn anything, what would you choose to learn about, and why?

How schools use the ISEE essay:

The way in which each admissions department uses the ISEE essay varies from school to school, but the following are the main essay elements that will be evaluated:

1. Topic choice
2. Organization and structure
3. Use of examples and details
4. Writing mechanics (spelling, punctuation, grammar)

Tip

Some schools will compare student application essays with the ISEE essay. If the application essays are written very differently from the ISEE essay, schools may disregard the application essays entirely based on an assumption that these may have been written by someone else (a parent, tutor, etc.)

Make sure that you write your own application essays! Parents, guardians, and others can help with the editing process, but the writing should be your own!

Chapter 3:

Preparing for the ISEE

Getting Ready for the Test

Now that you know the specifics of the ISEE, knowing how to be confident and ready to succeed on test day all comes down to your practice.

The Top 5 Reasons to Prepare:

1. The ISEE is a unique test.

The format and content of the ISEE differ significantly from that of other standardized tests you may have taken previously. Knowing what to expect on test day is the most important reason to prepare. Preparation helps relieve testing anxiety and ensures that you are already familiar with the types of questions on the test, so there are no surprises on test day.

2. The ISEE is a long test.

Sitting for so long is already an inherent challenge. Building up test-taking stamina will help you to stay focused for the duration of the test.

3. The ISEE is a competitive test.

It is taken only by students applying to competitive private schools and is designed to distinguish excellent students from a pool of above-average students.

4. The ISEE is a challenging test.

This is especially true for students at the younger end of the age range for any given level of the test. Simply knowing how to remain calm when presented with unfamiliar content is an important skill.

5. The ISEE is a learning opportunity.

The ISEE provides a concrete goal and clear learning objectives for students. It gives them an opportunity to set goals, practice, and achieve, just as they might in sports or music. Regardless of students' academic journeys or ultimate career paths, the skills they learn in practicing for the ISEE will serve them well in the future.

Preparation Basics

Practice timeline:

In general, the earlier you start, the better. If you can give yourself at least six months, that is ideal – having more time relieves the anxiety of trying to rush any learning. However, it is never too late to start practicing. The more you know about the test structure and questions, the better you will do. We've seen students massively improve in just a week by understanding how the test is structured and what's expected of them.

In terms of practice frequency and duration, this is very student-dependent, as most learning is. Our main advice is to focus on consistency and quality. For consistency, practice regularly even if not for a long period of time. One hour once a week is much more effective than four hours once a month. For each study session, if you can no longer learn new material because you've been sitting for so long, it's a good idea to take a break. (Though also see the tip below about full-length practice tests.)

Practice format:

We recommend that you practice both online and on paper.

Paper practice is important if you are taking the official test on paper. In particular, it is crucial to practice using the answer sheet to bubble in answers. It is better for you to have a bubbling snafu on the practice test than to make that mistake on the official test.

Computer practice is important if you are taking the official test on a computer. If you are taking the official test on paper, online practice is still important for timing feedback, one of the key strategic areas of this test.

Tip

Every level of the ISEE requires stamina and focus. Sit for a full-length practice test before the official one so that you know how it feels! Use a virtual proctor to simulate the official test:

https://testinnovators.com/proctor-videos

How to Prepare

Step 1: Take a full-length practice test.

This initial practice test serves as a benchmark, or diagnostic test, and is the jumping-off point of the preparation process. We generally recommend taking this test as early as possible, but it is never too late.

No matter how close it is to your official test date, taking a practice test will familiarize you with the test's style, difficulty, and content so that you know what to expect on test day.

The most important thing about a practice test is its accuracy – if the practice test does not reflect the content of the official test well, the benefits of taking that practice test are limited. There are many sample tests and practice resources available, and we encourage you to research them. We have spent a great deal of time making our practice as accurate as possible, and we continually ask for feedback every year to make sure our content is up to date. You can find our practice materials at https:// ISEEpracticetest.com

Step 2: Identify strengths and weaknesses based on results.

Look at overall trends first. Which sections went well, and which sections would you like to improve? Then dig deeper. What specific question types or subject areas went well, and which ones could use improvement? Do geometry concepts need brushing up, or are the algebra problems tripping you up?

At this point, consider time management as well. Did you manage your time effectively on each section? Did you run out of time to answer all of the questions on any of the sections?

Tip

Make sure that you have access to normative scores for your practice tests! Remember that answering 75% of the questions correctly on a given section may be a great score or an average score depending on the grade level and difficulty of the section.

Step 3: Focus on any weak areas identified in Step 2.

This is the step at which all of the learning takes place! Review every question that you answered incorrectly or skipped. Make sure that you would know how to answer them correctly if you saw them again. This means that you should not only know why the correct answer is correct, but also why the answer you chose (and the other incorrect answers) is wrong.

For verbal questions, add words you don't know to your vocabulary list. This includes words from the answer choices.

For math questions, identify the concepts and skills being tested in the questions you missed. Study those concepts, starting with the topics and question types you have seen before but may need review. After mastering those, delve into the unfamiliar content.

For reading questions, practice finding textual evidence (see reading strategies for more information): find line numbers to support every correct answer, and determine what information in the passage made each incorrect answer wrong.

To help students practice specific skills, we have additional practice exercises linked to each question so that students can follow up with relevant work. Whatever materials you choose to work with, be sure to include targeted practice of the specific question types you are missing. This approach will be much more impactful than simply taking full-length test sections. To help students practice specific skills, our practice tests have additional practice exercises linked to each test question.

Step 4: Take another full-length practice test, and repeat.

The preparation process is an iterative one. Each practice test should serve as a benchmark of progress. Studying between practice tests allows you to see growth and improvement between tests.

After you have reviewed and reflected on test results, learn everything about the questions you missed, and then take another practice to gauge your progress and determine what you need to work on next.

Chapter 4:

Strategies for the ISEE

Overall ISEE
Test-Taking Strategies

Process of Elimination

The ISEE is a multiple-choice test, so even if you aren't sure about the correct answer, you should still be thinking about whether there are answer choices that you know are wrong. After eliminating wrong answers, you can make an educated guess. In fact, elimination is sometimes all you need to find the right answer!

Read the specific strategies for each section to learn ways to eliminate answer choices for different question types.

This is a sample ISEE question. Don't forget to think about which answer choices you can eliminate as you solve this problem!

(A)   Definitely wrong answer
(B)   Possible answer
(C)   Possible answer
(D)   Definitely wrong answer

Guessing

On the ISEE, correct answers are awarded 1 point, and blank answers receive 0 points. There is no wrong-answer penalty, so you should always answer every question. Whenever possible, eliminate as many answer choices as you can before guessing, to increase your chances of answering correctly. That said, if you encounter a question where you cannot eliminate any answer choices, or if you are running out of time in the section, you should still select an answer choice for every question!

Time Management

Using your time effectively on the ISEE is critical. Every correct answer gives you the same number of points, so your goal is to answer as many questions correctly as possible. Don't waste valuable time on a hard question when you could instead answer three easy questions correctly in the same amount of time.

Here are three steps to manage your time well:

1. Group questions by difficulty: easy and hard. What does that mean? Every time you read a question, ask yourself "do I know how to do this?" If the answer is "Yes, absolutely" – solve the question. If the answer is "Maybe" or "I'm really not sure about this," or as you start the problem, you realize that it's taking you a long time, skip it.

2. When you skip a question, mark an answer on your answer sheet and circle the question on your test booklet. Filling in an answer on your answer sheet will ensure that you don't mis-bubble your answers!

3. After going through the whole section, return to the hard questions you marked and see if you can make any progress.

This is an example of what timing feedback looks like in our system:

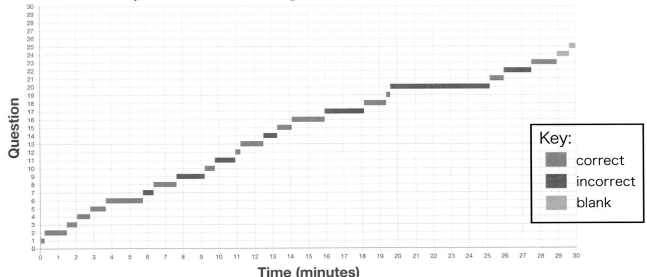

You can see that this student spent far too long on question 20, and therefore didn't have time to answer all of the questions. Insights like these are critical to building effective time management skills.

Verbal Strategies

Study vocabulary

If you have more than two weeks to prepare for the ISEE, studying vocabulary is a very good idea! The verbal section largely relies on knowledge of words, so the more words you know, the better.

Study vocabulary for 10-15 minutes every day – short, consistent study sessions are the best way to effectively build vocabulary.

You can find good word lists for each ISEE level here:

https://quizlet.com/testinnovators/folders

Think of your own answer first

Always think of your own answer before looking at the answer choices. You should use this strategy for both the synonym questions and the sentence completion questions.

Coming up with your own answer first is the best way to avoid tempting wrong answers that are related to the question, but do not have the correct meaning.

Don't worry about coming up with a perfect word for either synonym questions or sentence completion questions. It's fine to think of a phrase or feeling that fits. For synonym questions, perhaps you can only think of a context, phrase, or sentence in which you've heard the word before. Anything helps!

Find the answer choice that is closest to the word or idea that you predicted.

Break words apart

If you encounter a word that is unfamiliar to you, see if you can break the word apart. Roots contain the core meaning of a word, and prefixes and suffixes supplement that meaning. Do you recognize part of the word? Do you know another word that has that part? If so, use it to help you predict the meaning of the given word, or to eliminate answer choices that are not in line with that meaning.

Here's an example of how to apply this strategy:

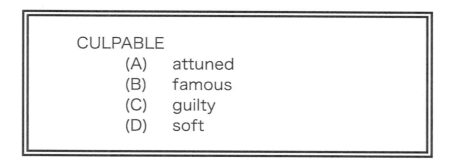

CULPABLE
- (A) attuned
- (B) famous
- (C) guilty
- (D) soft

Try breaking the word apart:

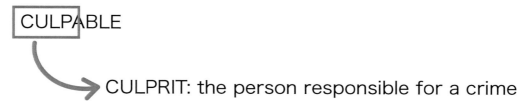

CULPABLE

CULPRIT: the person responsible for a crime

Although you may not have known the word culpable, you might know the word culprit. Using that, you can choose the answer choice closest to this meaning, which is C: guilty.

Use word connotation

Connotation is the mood or feeling associated with a word. Sometimes, you might not know what a word means, and you might not recognize parts of it, but you can still figure out if it is a good thing or a bad thing. To use this strategy, assign words a sign: positive, negative, or neutral.

For synonym questions, the sign of the given word should match the sign of the correct answer. For sentence completions, the sign that should go in the blank should match the sign of the correct answer.

Here's an example of how you might apply this strategy to a synonym question:

> SINISTER → −
> (A)   grand → +
> (B)   menacing → −
> (C)   perky → +
> (D)   unseen → neutral

Here's an example of how you might apply this strategy to a sentence completion:

> It is the unattractive appearance of the institution, with its dingy walls and ghastly lighting, that ------- visitors young and old.
> (A)   convinces → +   ↳ −
> (B)   fascinates → +
> (C)   inspires → +
> (D)   repels → −

Underline in sentence completions

As you read each sentence, underline the words that give you clues about what will go in the blank. Words that tell you the type of sentence are helpful, such as "however," "although," "because," or "not." Also underline words that give you the meaning of the sentence: the critical adjectives and nouns that indicate what the sentence is talking about.

Here are a few examples of how to underline the most important words in a sentence completion:

<u>Unlike</u> orangutans, which are ------- primates, gorillas are <u>social</u> apes and <u>live in groups</u> referred to as "troops."

John and Keaton were told the rental cabin would be <u>fully stocked with food</u> for their ski weekend, <u>but</u> when they arrived they found the contents of the <u>refrigerator</u> to be -------.

The Komodo dragon <u>does not</u> have a(n) ------- sense of hearing, <u>which is why</u> scientists originally believed the species to be <u>deaf</u>.

Math Strategies

Read carefully

One of the most common mistakes on the ISEE is misreading a question, usually due to reading too quickly. Be sure to take a few extra seconds on every question to avoid careless errors.

Underline important information.

This includes words and numbers indicating the quantities, relationships, and calculations (less than, twice, product, etc.) that you'll need to answer the question. Words like "not" can be easily missed and completely change what you're supposed to find in the question!

Here's an example of underlining:

> Whitney has taken three quizzes in her French class so far, earning scores of <u>84, 92, and 88</u>. Her next <u>test score</u> will be counted <u>three times in her overall mean</u>. If she takes only these three quizzes and one test, <u>what is the lowest score</u> she can earn on the test to have a <u>mean score of at least 90</u>?

Check that you answered the given question.

For every problem, after you finish solving, look back at what the question was asking you to find. Make sure that this matches your answer.

Here's an example of this check:

> Carla and Teresa are each taking turns driving a car. Carla drives 4 times as much as Teresa. If Carla and Teresa drive a total of 220 miles, how many miles did Teresa drive?

It would be easy to accidentally solve for the number of miles Carla drove, which will almost certainly be one of the answer choices as a common error. Take the extra second to verify that the question is asking for Teresa's miles, and answer accordingly.

Work backwards

Take advantage of the fact that the ISEE gives you more information than just a question: it also gives you answer choices, one of which you know must be the correct answer!

For questions with an unknown quantity, you can substitute the answer choices for the unknown quantity to see which is correct. Always start with the middle answer choice to minimize the number of answers you have to substitute.

A farmyard has 17 chickens and pigs in it, and 52 total feet. Assuming that all of the chickens have two feet, and all of the pigs have four, how many chickens are in the yard?

    (A)   7
    (B)   8
    (C)   9
    (D)   10

This is a tricky question to solve directly, but substituting answer choices is very manageable. Remember to start with one of the middle answer choices. Let's try C: 9.

If there are 9 chickens, then there must be 8 pigs. The total number of feet will be $9 \cdot 2 + 8 \cdot 4 = 18 + 32 = 50$. This is too few feet, so C is incorrect. To increase the number of feet, we must have fewer chickens and more pigs, so D must also be incorrect and we should try B: 8 next.

If there are 8 chickens, then there must be 9 pigs. The total number of feet will be $8 \cdot 2 + 9 \cdot 4 = 16 + 36 = 52$.

B is the correct answer.

Estimate

Estimation is a powerful tool for eliminating wrong answers. For every question, before beginning to solve, ballpark what you think the right answer should be. Think about things like: should it be positive or negative, an integer or a fraction, bigger or smaller than any of the other numbers in the question, and so on. Sometimes the question will even include clues that you should estimate, such as "approximately" or "about," but even without these words, always estimate first.

Here is an example of how to use estimation:

If 5/6 of a chapter can be read in one hour, how many hours will it take to read the rest of the chapter at the same rate?

    (A)   0.14
    (B)   0.20
    (C)   1.20
    (D)   1.83

Notice that the question is asking how long it will take to read the REST of the chapter. Since almost the entire chapter has been read already, it cannot possibly take more than an hour to read the remainder, so you can immediately eliminate answer choices C and D.

Thus, even with very little time spent on this question, you have a 50% chance of answering correctly.

Pick values

Sometimes, the math questions you see on the Quantitative Reasoning and Math Achievement sections may seem very challenging to solve abstractly. The question may ask how an unknown quantity will change if it undergoes a couple of percent changes, or to solve for one variable in terms of others. In cases like these, it can be helpful to use actual numbers to determine the answer, rather than trying to solve algebraically.

Here is an example of how to use this strategy:

If the length of the base of a triangle is decreased by 40% and the height is increased by 60%, what is the percent decrease in the area of the triangle?

    (A)   4%
    (B)   20%
    (C)   24%
    (D)   36%

Pick easy values for the base and height of the triangle, say 10 and 20. Thus the initial area of the triangle is $0.5 \cdot 10 \cdot 20 = 100$. (We chose these numbers strategically so that the area would be 100.)

Now the base decreases 40%, so the new base is 6, and the height increases 60%, so the new height is 32. Thus the new area of the triangle is $0.5 \cdot 6 \cdot 32 = 96$.

Therefore, the area of the triangle has decreased 4%.

Note: For percent questions, use 10% as your guide. 10% of any number is that number divided by 10, which is the same as moving the decimal point one unit to the left. Thus 10% of 60 is 6, 10% of 72 is 7.2, and so on.

Reading Strategies

Find evidence

The most important rule of reading comprehension is that the answer is always in the passage. This means that reading comprehension is really like a scavenger hunt, and your objective is to get as good as possible at sleuthing, finding the lines that give the answer to the question as quickly as possible.

If any part of an answer choice doesn't match the information given in the passage, it is incorrect. Even one word can make an answer choice wrong!

The correct answer should always have the same meaning as the information in the passage.

Think of your own answer first

Whenever possible, after you read a question, come up with an answer in your head before you look at the answer choices. This will help you to eliminate wrong answer choices, and find the best answer.

Eliminate extreme answers

In general, avoid answer choices that are too extreme. ISEE passages are usually moderate in their claims. If you see answer choices with words like "only," "always," "never," "best," "every," or other extreme words, these are unlikely to be the correct answer. You should only choose them if you are absolutely sure that this sentiment is in the passage as well.

Main idea strategy

After reading the passage, come up with the main idea in your own words. What was the passage all about? Start by eliminating answer choices that are not in line with your main idea. If you're torn between a couple of answer choices, determine how many lines of the passage talk about each answer choice. The one that covers more of the passage is a better answer.

Tone strategy

Tone questions ask how an author feels about the information in the passage. Start by determining if the tone is positive, negative, or neutral. To help decide, pay attention to adjectives and other charged/feeling words in the passage. Find the answer that best matches the way the author is talking about the subject.

Note: Neutral tone answer choices may be "informative" or "factual." A persuasive tone is indicated by words like "should" "ought to" "must" and "need."

Vocabulary in context strategy

Treat these questions like sentence completions. Don't look at the answer choices at first. Instead go to the line in question, read the sentence (covering up the word), and come up with your own word to go in the blank. Then find the closest answer choice. Afterwards, plug your answer into the sentence and make sure that it fits.

Essay Strategies

Topic choice

Try to choose a topic that showcases something you care about and are familiar with. Remember to write in a way that shows you in a positive light, and that highlights part of your personality. This is your chance to show the school who you are outside of school!

For example, imagine that you are given this prompt:

> If you were granted the power to move anywhere in the world, where would you decide to live and why?

Make sure to pick a topic that is personally important to you! Is there a place you have visited that has meant a lot to you, or a place where people that you care about live? Make sure to choose something you know about, care about, and can tell stories about.

Essay structure

For the personal essay, you should have a clear, focused topic that directly answers the given question. It should be structured much like essays you've written in school—include an introduction, two or three body paragraphs, and a conclusion.

In the introduction, state your topic and then introduce your 2-3 reasons – these will be the topics of your body paragraphs. In the body paragraphs, include specific examples from your experiences to support each of these reasons. Then, in the conclusion, rephrase your main points and offer something new to the reader, such as describing how this topic will affect your actions in the future.

Time management

With limited time to write, managing your time effectively is incredibly important. Start by spending the first 2-5 minutes outlining your work. After you have a plan, go ahead and get writing! This is where you will spend the bulk of your time. You'll need to watch the clock, and save yourself 2-5 minutes at the end for review.

Examples and details

The magic is in the details! Your writing should include examples and specific details that make your writing come alive. The body of your writing should draw on details and stories from your life so that the reader can get to know you better.

If you are writing about a place you'd want to move, for example, tell about an important visit you had there. Describe the scenery and the sights and sounds! Use words that appeal to the reader's senses: sight, sound, smell, touch, and taste.

Revision

Editing and reviewing at the end is a crucial step in creating a polished writing sample.

Try to catch any grammar, spelling, capitalization, or punctuation mistakes, and change "weak" words to "strong" ones. Instead of, "I walked to the beach," write, "I strolled leisurely to the beach," or "I dashed down the path to the beach."

Neatness and organization matter! You want your writing to be as smooth and polished as possible. Make sure you write slowly enough that your handwriting is legible.

Chapter 5:

Conclusion

How to prepare from here

This book should serve as a guide and introduction to the ISEE and best preparation practices. Remember that practice is the cornerstone of the preparation process!

The next thing to do is to take practice tests and do practice questions. Apply the strategies covered in Chapter 4 until they are second nature.

There are many resources available with ISEE practice. We have spent a great deal of time developing quality practice materials, and you can access these at ISEEpracticetest.com

You can use the coupon code GUIDEBOOK for $25 off any Valedictorian package.

If you have any questions about the preparation process, don't hesitate to reach out to us! From September through January, we have someone answering the phone and responding to emails 7 days a week. Outside of the core testing season, we are available Monday through Friday to answer your questions. Our contact information is:

PHONE: 1-800-280-1857
EMAIL: support@testinnovators.com

We wish you the best of luck in the preparation process!

Good Luck!

Made in the USA
San Bernardino, CA
04 February 2019